CONTENTS

Spartacus - A Tale of Defiance, Freedom, and Courage	1
The Legend of Spartacus	2
The Birth of a Gladiator	4
The Brutality of Roman Slavery	9
The Escape from Capua	15
Building an Army of the Oppressed	22
The First Victories	29
Defying the Roman Legions	37
A Dream of Freedom	45
The Brutal Endgame	52
The Last Stand	59
Spartacus's Legacy	66
The Eternal Flame of Rebellion	73
ABOUT THE AUTHOR	78

SPARTACUS - A TALE OF DEFIANCE, FREEDOM, AND COURAGE

Ciro Irmici

Copyright © 2024 Ciro Irmici

All rights reserved.

THE LEGEND OF SPARTACUS

In the shadow of the mighty Roman Empire, a legend was born. The tale of Spartacus, the Thracian gladiator who rose against the most formidable power of his time, has endured through centuries. It is a story not just of warfare, but of hope, defiance, and the unbreakable human spirit. Spartacus's journey from slave to rebel leader stands as one of history's most profound symbols of resistance against oppression.

The Rome of Spartacus's era was a paradox—a society that thrived on intellectual achievement, military might, and architectural splendor, yet depended on an economy built upon the backs of slaves. Enslaved men and women formed the foundation of the empire's prosperity, but they were often brutalized, dehumanized, and forced into grueling labor. Among them was Spartacus, a warrior who refused to accept the chains of servitude. Captured and sold as a gladiator, Spartacus found himself facing a life where his strength and spirit were nothing more than a spectacle for the Roman elite.

Yet, Spartacus was not born to live as someone else's property. His defiance sparked a rebellion that would shake Rome to its core. With remarkable skill and charisma, he inspired an army of the oppressed—men and women from every background and nation bound together by their desire for freedom. What began as a desperate escape from a gladiator school in Capua transformed into a revolutionary war, a fight for dignity that Rome could neither ignore nor easily crush.

This book will explore the life of Spartacus and his rebellion, diving into the battles, sacrifices, and ideals that drove his followers. We will unravel the complex societal structures that allowed such widespread oppression and examine how one man's rebellion exposed the empire's greatest fears. We will follow Spartacus and his unlikely army as they defy legion after legion, challenging the might of Rome and leaving a legacy that endures far beyond the bloodstained fields of ancient Italy.

Through this journey, we will ask important questions: What compels a person to risk everything for freedom? How does a movement of the oppressed organize, resist, and ultimately inspire? Spartacus's story, while historical, is ultimately a timeless reminder that even the most powerful oppressors can be challenged by the courage of those they underestimate.

THE BIRTH OF A GLADIATOR

Long before he became a name that sent shivers through the Roman Republic, Spartacus was a young Thracian boy growing up on the wild, rugged edges of the known world. Thrace, a region to the north of Greece and east of the Danube River, was a land marked by fierce independence, where clans held fast to their traditions and warrior culture. Spartacus's early years in Thrace would shape him, instilling in him the resilience, physical strength, and fierce loyalty to freedom that would later define his rebellion. To understand Spartacus, we must first understand the world that shaped him—a place where honor and survival were inseparable and where the spirit of defiance ran as deep as the rivers carving through Thrace's mountains.

A Warrior's Beginnings

As a young man in Thrace, Spartacus would have been trained in the ways of battle from an early age. Thracians were known throughout the ancient world for their prowess as warriors. Their unique fighting style, reliant on speed, agility, and close-range combat, contrasted with the more disciplined, formation-based tactics of the Roman legions. Spartacus likely trained with the curved sica, a short, viciously sharp blade suited to quick and deadly strikes. Thracian warriors were also known to fight with a ferocity that intimidated their foes. They were accustomed to raids, skirmishes, and close encounters, skills that would later aid Spartacus in his remarkable guerrilla campaign against Rome.

Despite their independence, the Thracians often found themselves at odds with the Roman Republic, which was expanding rapidly across Europe, subjugating entire nations in its path. While some Thracians resisted fiercely, others entered treaties with Rome, even enlisting as auxiliaries in the Roman military in exchange for a degree of autonomy or economic support. Spartacus's own people were no strangers to this arrangement, and he himself would eventually serve as a Roman auxiliary—a fateful decision that would lead him straight into captivity.

Captured and Enslaved

How exactly Spartacus became a slave remains a topic of historical debate, as ancient sources provide conflicting accounts. Some suggest that Spartacus deserted the Roman army, while others imply that he may have fallen into captivity after a failed raid or rebellion. Either way, what is known is that his capture marked a profound turning point in his life. He was bound, shackled, and sold into slavery—a brutal fate for any freeborn Thracian warrior. The Romans, ever efficient in exploiting their captives, decided Spartacus would make an ideal gladiator.

Spartacus was taken to the gladiator school, or ludus, in Capua, a Roman town infamous for its training facilities where men were conditioned to fight to the death for the entertainment of the public. His identity, like that of all slaves, was stripped away, replaced by the cold, calculated label of property. But Spartacus's spirit was not one to be subdued by chains or Roman authority. Even in captivity, he found ways to endure, to maintain his strength and courage, and to build connections with others suffering under the same yoke.

Life in the Gladiator School

Life in the ludus was nothing short of brutal. Gladiators were treated as disposable assets, their lives governed by the whims of their trainers and the hunger of Roman audiences for spectacle. Each day began with grueling physical drills, sparring matches, and intensive weapons training, designed to prepare them for the bloodshed of the arena. Their meals were carefully regulated, enough to maintain their physical strength but not enough to promote any sense of comfort or satisfaction. They lived in close quarters, their barracks filled with men from various regions who, like Spartacus, had been torn from their homes and forced into servitude.

The gladiators were trained in various fighting styles, depending on their origins, physique, and skills. Spartacus was likely trained as a Thraex, or Thracian-style gladiator, which would have allowed him to use the fighting techniques he knew well, albeit with specific rules and weapons suited for the arena. He was armed with a small, rectangular shield and a curved Thracian sword, meant for quick, cutting strikes. This role would have been bitterly ironic for Spartacus—forced to use his homeland's techniques, not for defense or honor, but for the amusement of Roman spectators.

Yet, even in this pit of despair, Spartacus found allies. Among them were Crixus and Oenomaus, both skilled fighters who shared his hatred for the Romans. Together, they harbored dreams of escape, a dangerous fantasy that could mean death if discovered. But Spartacus was no ordinary man; he was born of a people who valued freedom above all else. In the bonds of friendship formed with fellow gladiators, he found the foundation of what would become an army of rebels.

The Spark of Rebellion

What motivated Spartacus to risk everything for freedom? Perhaps it was the humiliation he endured as a captive, or the pride that burned within him as a Thracian warrior. Perhaps he saw himself in his fellow gladiators, men stripped of their dignity, their names, their homes. To the Romans, they were little more than animals, but to Spartacus, they were soldiers in waiting, each one capable of wielding a weapon, each one harboring a desire for freedom as strong as his own.

In this grim environment, Spartacus began to plan. He watched the movements of the guards, studied the layout of the ludus, and evaluated the strength of his comrades. The risks were enormous—escape attempts were usually met with swift and brutal punishment, not just for the instigators, but for all involved. Yet Spartacus knew that the only way to reclaim their lives was to break free from the chains holding them. A bold plan began to take shape, one that would test their courage and cunning to the limit.

The Night Before the Revolt

The night before the rebellion, Spartacus gathered his closest allies. The atmosphere was thick with tension, a silent understanding passing between them that the next day would either grant them freedom or see them dead. They knew they were vastly outnumbered and outarmed, yet they also knew they had one critical advantage: desperation. With no future in captivity, the fear of death no longer restrained them. They were ready to fight.

Using makeshift weapons fashioned from kitchen utensils, pieces of wood, and any sharp objects they could scavenge, Spartacus and his men prepared to take on the guards. It was a desperate move, and they knew it. But what they lacked in weaponry, they made up for in skill, determination, and the element of surprise.

The Morning of the Rebellion

At dawn, the signal was given. Spartacus and his allies launched their attack with precision, speed, and a fury that caught the guards completely off guard. The uprising quickly escalated as gladiators poured out of their cells, joining the fight. The rebellion spread like wildfire, and within hours, Spartacus and his men had overpowered the guards and escaped from the ludus of Capua.

Their initial victory was as unexpected as it was overwhelming, and it gave Spartacus and his men a taste of what freedom felt like. For the first time, they were no longer slaves but free men—armed, determined, and led by a man who had dared to defy the greatest power in the world. Spartacus knew, however, that the journey had only just begun. The Roman legions would soon be on their trail, and every step forward would be fraught with danger.

The Birth of a Movement

What began as an escape plan by a few desperate men would soon become one of the most formidable rebellions Rome had ever faced. Spartacus was no longer merely a gladiator or a slave; he was now a leader, a symbol of defiance for the oppressed. The gladiator school at Capua had forged in him a strength that no training could diminish, and now, with his followers at his side, he would unleash that strength against Rome itself.

THE BRUTALITY OF ROMAN SLAVERY

To understand the rebellion of Spartacus, we must delve into the institution he rebelled against: Roman slavery, a vast and oppressive system that fueled the power and wealth of the empire. The Rome of Spartacus's time was a sprawling empire, built on conquest and sustained by the labor of millions of enslaved people from every corner of the known world. For the Romans, slavery was not just an institution but a way of life, deeply embedded in every social, economic, and political aspect of their society.

For those trapped in this system, however, life was harsh and often unbearably cruel. Enslaved people were stripped of their rights, their identities, and their families, subjected to lives that were brutal, short, and filled with unimaginable hardship. Spartacus's rebellion was not merely a revolt by gladiators but a symbolic uprising of the enslaved against the inhuman treatment imposed upon them. This chapter will explore the brutal realities of Roman slavery, the different forms it took, and the constant, quiet resistance of those who dreamed of freedom.

The Scope of Roman Slavery

In the first century BCE, slaves made up a significant portion of Rome's population. Estimates suggest that between a quarter and a third of the population in major cities like Rome and Capua were enslaved. Enslaved people came from all walks of life and regions —from the skilled artisans and intellectuals of Greece to the fierce warriors of Gaul and the laborers of North Africa. Conquered peoples were often transported across the empire in massive numbers, torn from their homes and families to be sold as property.

These individuals found themselves integrated into every aspect of Roman life. Some labored in the harshest conditions on agricultural estates known as latifundia, while others were assigned to households as cooks, cleaners, or caretakers. Wealthy Romans displayed their power through the number and quality of slaves they owned, each one a symbol of the master's wealth and status. Roman society treated these human beings as commodities, with each slave given a price tag based on their physical strength, beauty, or skill. It was a system designed to break individuals and reinforce the hierarchy that kept Rome thriving.

The Different Lives of Slaves: Fields, Mines, and Households

Not all slaves suffered equally; their experiences varied drastically depending on their roles and their masters. At the bottom of the hierarchy were the servi vincti, those condemned to work in the mines or quarries. Life expectancy for these individuals was shockingly low, as they endured grueling labor in dark, suffocating conditions, breathing dust that damaged their lungs and enduring heat that left them exhausted and dehydrated. Few survived more than a few years in these conditions, as their bodies wore out quickly, and replacements were readily available from new conquests.

On agricultural estates, enslaved people worked under the

relentless sun, planting, harvesting, and maintaining crops that fed the empire. These estates were often overseen by harsh overseers who pushed them to their physical limits. These laborers lived in squalid, cramped conditions and were given minimal food and rest. Their lives were spent in a continuous cycle of back-breaking labor, deprived of any hope for a future beyond the fields.

In wealthier households, some slaves experienced slightly better treatment, but their lives were no less controlled. Household slaves could find themselves attending to the whims of their masters, from preparing meals to acting as tutors for children, performing any number of personal services. For female slaves, life in the household often included the threat of sexual abuse from their masters, with no legal recourse. Yet, even the most skilled slaves—tutors, musicians, or doctors—were still property, subject to sale or punishment at their owner's discretion.

Dehumanization and Control: How Rome Kept Slaves Subjugated

The Roman slave system was built not only on physical control but also on psychological oppression. Rome devised numerous strategies to strip enslaved people of their identities, making them feel powerless and isolated. Slaves were often given new names, stripping them of their former identities and cultures. They were also forbidden from legally marrying, and their families could be torn apart at any time. Children born to enslaved parents were automatically enslaved themselves, reinforcing a cycle of bondage that spanned generations.

Masters wielded absolute power over their slaves and could enforce discipline through any means they deemed necessary. Public floggings, starvation, and confinement were common punishments for any perceived disobedience. In severe cases, slaves were executed in brutal public displays, reinforcing their status as property without rights. The Romans used these measures to instill fear, discouraging slaves from rebelling or attempting escape.

Roman law provided virtually no protections for enslaved people, viewing them as property rather than human beings. A master could punish, sell, or even kill a slave without legal repercussions. Roman writers like Seneca and Cicero wrote about the moral responsibilities of masters, but these ideas were rarely put into practice. Rome's laws favored property rights over human rights, creating a legal system that sanctioned cruelty in the name of control.

Small Acts of Defiance

Despite the overwhelming oppression they faced, enslaved people found ways to resist. Open rebellion was rare, given the brutal consequences, but resistance took on many other forms. Some slaves would feign illness or sabotage work, slowing down productivity as a way of reclaiming a small piece of power over their lives. Others secretly maintained their cultural practices, preserving the languages, traditions, and beliefs of their homelands despite Rome's efforts to erase their identities.

In some cases, slaves forged close bonds with each other, creating a sense of family and community where none officially existed. These relationships were a source of emotional support and resilience, providing strength in a world that sought to dehumanize them. The small moments of solidarity and shared laughter, the secret exchanges of stories from their homelands, and the quiet acts of defiance were, in themselves, an assertion of their humanity.

However, the idea of a large-scale rebellion remained a distant hope for most, a dream that felt impossible under the weight of Roman oppression. That is, until Spartacus emerged. In him, the slaves saw a leader who could articulate the pain and anger they all felt, a warrior who dared to dream of a life free from Roman chains.

The Gladiator Schools: Preparing Men for Battle or Death

The gladiator schools like the one in Capua, where Spartacus was trained, represented a unique blend of cruelty and survival. The Roman elite viewed gladiators as living entertainment, men who would fight to the death in arenas for the crowds. But to the men forced into this role, the schools were both a prison and a training ground, where the skills they learned would prove invaluable in their fight for freedom.

Gladiators, especially those with military experience like Spartacus, were seen as prime candidates for rebellion due to their combat skills. The training was rigorous, preparing them not just to survive in the arena but to fight effectively against other skilled warriors. Gladiators were conditioned to endure pain, withstand brutal conditions, and confront death with courage. For many, the training they endured became a source of pride and resilience, a skill set that would soon turn against the very society that had crafted it.

The Seed of Revolt

As Spartacus trained alongside men from various backgrounds—Gauls, Germans, Africans, Greeks—a bond began to form among them. They shared the same brutal circumstances, the same exhaustion, the same anger. Despite the guards and the punishments, a growing undercurrent of rebellion simmered among the gladiators. They whispered of escape, exchanging glances that spoke volumes when words were too dangerous.

Spartacus's experience as a soldier and his natural leadership qualities drew others to him, and soon he became the unspoken leader of the discontent within the gladiator school. It was here that the idea of rebellion transformed from a quiet dream into a concrete plan. This defiance was not just about escaping from Capua—it was about challenging the entire Roman system that exploited them, an empire built on their suffering.

The Rising Tide of Discontent

The life of a slave was one of despair, but it was also one filled with a simmering anger, an anger that Spartacus tapped into with astonishing effectiveness. In him, they saw not only a leader but a man who understood their pain and shared their dreams of freedom. The brutality of Roman slavery had created the perfect conditions for a rebellion; it was a tinderbox waiting for a spark. And Spartacus, with his vision and courage, was that spark.

As word of Spartacus's plans began to spread, he found himself at the head of a movement that would grow beyond the walls of Capua, beyond the reaches of the gladiator schools, and beyond the grasp of Rome itself. This rebellion was more than an escape—it was the birth of a movement that challenged Rome's very foundation, a force of human will driven by the shared memory of suffering and the undying hope for liberation.

The Romans had underestimated the resilience of those they enslaved, and in Spartacus, they faced not just a rebel but a symbol of all the lives they had disregarded. The brutality of Roman slavery had, inadvertently, forged an army of the determined—a force that would soon rise to defy the empire, one battle at a time.

THE ESCAPE FROM CAPUA

The gladiator school at Capua, the site of Spartacus's first act of open defiance, was a fortress of despair for most, a place where men were trained to kill for the entertainment of the Roman elite. Yet, within those bleak walls, Spartacus and his comrades saw a chance for liberation, a way to reclaim their lives and dignity. What started as whispers of escape soon grew into a carefully planned revolt, a desperate gamble that would see Spartacus and his allies break free and launch a rebellion that would shake the Roman Republic to its core.

This chapter chronicles the fateful escape from Capua—the planning, the rising anticipation, and the pivotal moments when Spartacus and his followers took up makeshift weapons and unleashed their fury. Their success that day would be the first of many, marking the beginning of a rebellion that Rome could neither ignore nor contain.

Capua: A Fortress and a Cage

The gladiator school in Capua, known as the ludus, was a formidable structure, heavily guarded and fortified to prevent any thoughts of escape. Located just south of Rome, Capua was famous for its arenas, where gladiators fought for the amusement of the public. The school's walls were high, the gates were fortified, and Roman guards patrolled the premises day and night. It was a place built not only to train gladiators but to contain them, to suppress any desire they might have for freedom.

The school was a grim, oppressive place where the enslaved gladiators were forced to live in squalid conditions, each day repeating the same grueling cycle of training, eating, and resting in preparation for their eventual fate in the arena. But despite the grim surroundings, a sense of camaraderie began to grow among the men. The shared suffering they endured forged bonds that transcended cultural and linguistic differences. Among the fighters were Gauls, Thracians, Germans, and others, each with their own story of how they had come to be captured, enslaved, and trained as gladiators.

For Spartacus, the school at Capua was more than a prison; it was a testament to Roman arrogance, a symbol of a society that thrived on the suffering of others. He despised the walls, the guards, and, most of all, the fate that awaited each of them. In his heart, Spartacus nurtured a growing anger, a smoldering resolve to break free. He began to look for weaknesses in the school's defenses, studying the movements of the guards, observing the routines that governed their captivity. In time, his plans grew more defined, his ambitions more daring.

The Conspiracy Takes Shape

The idea of escape was perilous. Spartacus knew the price of failure: torture and death, not only for him but for anyone involved. Roman guards were brutal in punishing escape attempts, using the severest measures to discourage dissent. Yet

Spartacus was no ordinary man. With his military background and natural leadership skills, he commanded respect among the other gladiators. They listened to him, trusted him, and many were willing to follow him, no matter the risk.

The plan began with a few select allies—men Spartacus knew he could trust implicitly. Crixus, a fierce Gaul, was one of the first to join him, a man whose strength and defiance made him an invaluable ally. Oenomaus, another skilled fighter, quickly joined the conspiracy. Together, they began recruiting others, carefully choosing those who had both the courage and the commitment to see the plan through.

As the plan developed, the conspirators scouted the school for any tools or weapons they could use. The gladiator school was, ironically, filled with weapons—swords, spears, and shields for training. However, these were kept locked away, heavily guarded by the trainers and overseers. Spartacus and his men realized they would need to improvise if they were to succeed. They fashioned makeshift weapons from kitchen tools, wooden clubs, and anything they could sharpen or use to inflict damage. The risk was enormous, but the rewards—freedom, life beyond the walls of Capua—were worth it.

The Tipping Point: The Day of Escape

The fateful day came unexpectedly. As the tension within the ludus built, rumors began to swirl that the guards had caught wind of an escape plan. Spartacus knew that if they delayed, they would likely be discovered and executed before they even had a chance to act. The time had come to make their move, and Spartacus seized the moment.

At dawn, he gave the signal. The conspirators moved swiftly, each one taking up a makeshift weapon and launching themselves at the guards with a fury born of desperation. What they lacked in armament, they made up for in skill and ferocity. Spartacus himself fought with a deadly determination, using a kitchen knife to subdue one of the guards and take his sword. His allies followed his lead, overwhelming the guards through sheer force of will and numbers.

The battle within the school was intense and chaotic. The guards, though armed, were unprepared for such an organized assault. They had always viewed the gladiators as nothing more than animals to be controlled, never imagining that these men could organize and execute such a bold plan. The gladiators fought with everything they had, fueled by the knowledge that there was no turning back. For each of them, this was a fight to the death—freedom or death.

As they pushed through the guards and made their way to the main gates, Spartacus and his men experienced a rush of exhilaration. The gates, once symbols of their confinement, now lay within their reach. They forced them open, spilling out of the ludus and into the open world. For the first time in years, they breathed the air of freedom. The city of Capua lay around them, its people unaware of the storm that had just been unleashed.

Rallying the Escapees: The Birth of a Rebel Army

Once outside the ludus, Spartacus knew that their escape was only the beginning. They had won their freedom, but they were still vulnerable, unarmed fugitives in the heart of Roman territory. Spartacus's first priority was to secure weapons and supplies for his newly liberated comrades. Fortunately, Capua was a town where many wealthy Romans lived, and it was not long before Spartacus and his followers located an estate where they could arm themselves.

In a daring raid, they overpowered the estate guards and seized weapons, armor, and provisions. For the first time, they were no longer makeshift warriors armed with kitchen utensils—they had real swords, shields, and a growing sense of purpose. Spartacus urged his men to move swiftly and quietly, gathering what they could before slipping into the nearby countryside, where they could plan their next steps and evade the inevitable Roman response.

As the days passed, more enslaved people began to hear of Spartacus's escape and joined him, swelling his numbers. His band of rebels grew rapidly, composed not only of escaped gladiators but of field slaves, household slaves, and others who had lived under the boot of Roman rule. Spartacus's army became a diverse group, united by a shared desire for freedom and a common hatred of Rome.

Rome Reacts: Underestimating the Rebellion

News of the escape spread quickly, and the Roman authorities in Capua were both alarmed and angered by the boldness of Spartacus's rebellion. To the Roman Senate, a band of runaway slaves was an insult, an affront to their authority and the carefully maintained social order. But initially, they did not view the rebellion as a serious threat. The Senate saw Spartacus and his men as a minor nuisance, a band of fugitives who could be easily subdued by a local militia or a small contingent of legionnaires.

Rome underestimated Spartacus's abilities, seeing him only as a former slave and a gladiator. They did not yet realize that he was also a skilled tactician with experience in warfare. The small detachments sent to capture him found themselves overwhelmed, outmatched by Spartacus's knowledge of guerrilla tactics and the ferocity of his followers. As his band won skirmish after skirmish, Spartacus's reputation grew, and more slaves began to flock to his cause, swelling his army and strengthening his resolve.

The First Victory: A Symbol of Hope

The first significant victory for Spartacus and his followers came in the hills near Capua. A Roman force, confident of an easy victory, attempted to corner Spartacus's group. But Spartacus, drawing on his military training and understanding of terrain, led his men in a surprise attack that shattered the Roman forces. It was a stunning defeat for the Romans, and it sent a powerful message to the people of Italy: Spartacus was not just a fugitive—he was a leader, and his followers were a formidable force.

This victory was more than just a tactical win; it was a profound moment of empowerment for Spartacus's followers. For the first time, they had not only escaped from Roman chains but had also defeated the very people who had oppressed them. News of this victory spread quickly, inspiring enslaved people across the region and frightening the Roman elite, who began to realize that Spartacus was more than just a renegade slave. He was a symbol of defiance, a man who dared to fight back against Rome.

Building a Movement

With each victory, Spartacus's numbers swelled. His followers included men, women, and even children, many of whom had endured years of suffering under Roman masters. What had started as a band of runaway gladiators was now transforming into a movement, a collective uprising of the oppressed. Spartacus treated his followers with respect, emphasizing equality and camaraderie—a stark contrast to the cruelty they had experienced under Roman rule.

As they moved through the countryside, Spartacus and his

followers left a trail of liberated slaves and humiliated Roman forces in their wake. They raided estates, redistributed resources, and gave hope to those who had long been denied it. Spartacus's army became a force of freedom, a growing coalition united by a shared dream of breaking free from Rome's iron grip.

A Dream of Freedom

Spartacus's rebellion was no longer just about escape; it was about creating a future where his followers could live free. He began to articulate a vision beyond mere survival—a vision where they could escape to the Alps and find refuge in lands beyond Rome's reach. This dream of freedom ignited the hearts of his followers, giving them a common goal and a purpose that transcended their individual sufferings.

As Spartacus led his army further into the Italian countryside, he knew that Rome would soon respond with greater force. But he was undeterred, driven by the same fire that had fueled his escape from Capua. He had defied Rome, rallied an army of the oppressed, and achieved victories that would echo through history.

In Capua, the rebellion had been born; now, it was unstoppable. The path forward was uncertain, but for Spartacus and his followers, the journey had only just begun.

BUILDING AN ARMY OF THE OPPRESSED

After the successful escape from Capua and the resounding victory against Roman forces in the hills, Spartacus found himself at the head of a growing band of rebels. What had begun as a desperate attempt at freedom was now transforming into a powerful, organized movement, fueled by a common vision and an unwavering resolve. Spartacus was no longer leading a small group of gladiators; he was the commander of an expanding force of men and women, united by a shared purpose and a desire for liberation. The task now was not just to survive but to build an army capable of challenging the might of Rome itself.

This chapter explores how Spartacus transformed a loosely connected band of fugitives into a disciplined force, instilling them with the tactics, morale, and vision necessary to confront the Roman military. It examines his leadership style, his innovative strategies, and the challenges he faced in uniting such a diverse group of people under a single cause.

Gathering the Dispossessed

Word of Spartacus's rebellion spread like wildfire. Enslaved people across the Italian countryside, some who had been living in bondage for decades, heard rumors of a Thracian gladiator who had escaped and was leading a growing rebellion against the Romans. For many, Spartacus became a symbol of hope—a living testament to the possibility of freedom in a world that had only shown them chains. Men and women from every corner of Italy fled their masters and joined Spartacus's ranks, swelling his numbers and transforming his band of fugitives into an army.

The diversity of Spartacus's followers was one of the greatest challenges he faced as a leader. His forces included former gladiators, agricultural slaves, miners, household servants, and even freedmen who were fed up with the cruelty of the Roman system. They came from different backgrounds, spoke different languages, and had little in common other than a shared hatred for Rome and a desire for freedom. Spartacus faced the daunting task of uniting them, turning this mass of people into a cohesive, organized force.

Training the Troops

Spartacus understood that if they were to survive the coming battles with Rome, his followers would need to be more than a mob; they would need to be disciplined soldiers. Drawing upon his experience as a former Roman auxiliary and a gladiator, he established a rigorous training regimen, teaching his recruits the fundamentals of combat, formation, and discipline. For many of his followers, this was the first time they had ever held a weapon or stood in a line with others, let alone prepared for a battle against a professional army. But Spartacus was a patient and inspiring leader, training them with a mixture of toughness and encouragement.

In addition to hand-to-hand combat, Spartacus trained his followers in guerrilla tactics—ambushes, surprise attacks, and quick retreats—methods that would allow them to take on larger, better-equipped Roman forces. He emphasized the importance of using the terrain to their advantage, teaching his soldiers how to fight in hills, forests, and open fields. He also devised signals and strategies that allowed his forces to communicate and move quickly, turning what could have been a chaotic mob into an agile, coordinated unit.

The training was brutal, and the conditions were harsh. Spartacus's camp was no place for the faint-hearted. Food was often scarce, and the soldiers lived in makeshift tents and shelters, enduring rain, cold, and heat. Yet, through this shared hardship, a sense of camaraderie developed among the soldiers. Spartacus treated them as equals, building a rapport that fostered loyalty and unity. The sense of purpose he instilled in them became a powerful motivator, transforming a group of enslaved people into a disciplined, determined force.

Forging a Community

While training his followers, Spartacus also recognized the importance of forging a community. His army was not just a fighting force but a diverse collection of families, friends, and companions bound together by their shared struggle. He encouraged them to form bonds, to look out for one another, and to see themselves not just as soldiers but as members of a larger cause. Children, the elderly, and the sick were all part of the camp, each contributing in their own way. Women took on roles as medics, cooks, and caretakers, while some even trained as warriors alongside the men.

Spartacus's followers were more than just soldiers; they were a society on the move, carrying their dreams, traditions, and hopes for the future. Around the campfires, they shared stories from their homelands, spoke of the families they had lost, and envisioned a life beyond the chains of slavery. These moments of community, the laughter and the shared pain, strengthened their resolve. Spartacus fostered this unity, understanding that an army bound by loyalty and brotherhood was far stronger than one bound merely by fear.

A Code of Conduct

To maintain order and discipline within the growing ranks, Spartacus established a simple but strict code of conduct. He emphasized respect, both for each other and for the people they encountered. Unlike the Roman forces, who often terrorized and plundered the countryside, Spartacus's army was instructed to treat local villages and their inhabitants with kindness and fairness. This approach won them the support of local communities, who, while wary of Spartacus's army, saw them as a lesser threat compared to the brutal Roman legions.

Spartacus was particularly strict about the treatment of women within his ranks, forbidding any form of harassment or abuse. This was revolutionary at the time, as Rome's treatment of enslaved women was often one of exploitation and objectification. In Spartacus's camp, however, women were treated as equal members of the community, and many took up arms alongside the men, fighting for their freedom with the same ferocity and determination.

Building Morale: The Vision of Freedom

One of the most critical aspects of Spartacus's leadership was his ability to inspire his followers with a vision of freedom. He spoke often of their goal—to cross the Alps and reach lands beyond Rome's reach, where they could live free from the empire's tyranny. This vision of freedom was more than just a dream; it was a guiding purpose, a beacon that kept them moving forward, even in the face of hardship and danger.

Spartacus's speeches to his followers were simple but powerful, emphasizing the value of freedom and the dignity of living as free people, not as property. He reminded them of the injustices they had suffered, of the lives they had been denied, and of the loved ones they had lost to Rome's insatiable greed. He called on them to fight not just for themselves, but for all those who could not fight —for the enslaved families, for the children who had been born into bondage, for the friends who had died under Rome's rule. Each soldier, each follower, felt that they were part of something greater than themselves—a movement that could change the course of history.

Clashes with Roman Forces

As Spartacus's army grew, the Roman Senate could no longer ignore him. They sent detachments to quash the rebellion, but Spartacus's training and tactics proved effective against the disciplined but rigid Roman legions. Spartacus led his army in a series of skirmishes and battles, outmaneuvering the Romans with his intimate knowledge of terrain and his strategic use of ambushes. He used the land to his advantage, luring Roman forces into traps, hitting them hard, and then melting away before they could mount a proper defense.

These victories were more than just military triumphs; they were acts of psychological warfare. Each time Spartacus's army defeated a Roman force, it sent a powerful message to Rome and to the oppressed people across Italy. Rome was not invincible. The rebellion was not a hopeless cause. With each victory, Spartacus's legend grew, and more enslaved people flocked to his ranks, eager to fight for a life beyond slavery.

The Challenges of Leadership

Despite his growing success, Spartacus faced constant challenges as a leader. His army was a diverse group, with members from different cultures, backgrounds, and beliefs. Conflicts occasionally arose, as former slaves from different regions clashed over differences in language, customs, and roles within the army. Some wanted immediate revenge against Roman citizens, while others were more focused on survival and escape. Spartacus had to navigate these conflicts carefully, maintaining unity while addressing the concerns of his followers.

Furthermore, Spartacus was well aware that they could not evade Rome's full military power indefinitely. He understood that Rome would eventually send its most skilled generals and its largest armies to crush the rebellion. The vision of crossing the Alps offered hope, but it also presented a significant logistical challenge. Moving such a large and diverse group through hostile territory was no small feat, and every day spent in Italy increased the risk of facing Rome's wrath.

The Seeds of Disagreement

As the rebellion grew, so did the internal disagreements about its direction. Some of Spartacus's followers, particularly the more aggressive fighters like Crixus, pushed for a direct assault on Rome. They argued that retreating across the Alps was cowardly and that they should use their momentum to strike at the heart of the empire. Spartacus, however, was cautious. He understood the limitations of their resources and the risk of overreaching. His goal remained simple: freedom beyond Rome's borders, not conquest or empire.

These disagreements hinted at future divisions within the ranks, but for the moment, Spartacus managed to hold his army together. He reminded his followers that their ultimate goal was not revenge but freedom. They were not conquerors; they were people fighting for their right to live with dignity.

Preparing for the Next Phase

By the end of this phase, Spartacus had achieved what many thought impossible: he had built an army from the ranks of the oppressed, a force capable of standing against the Roman legions and winning. They were disciplined, united by purpose, and inspired by a vision of freedom that kept them moving forward. Yet, Spartacus knew that the journey ahead would only grow more challenging. Rome was beginning to understand the threat he posed, and he could sense that a greater force would soon come to confront them.

For now, Spartacus and his followers pressed on, with the Alps as their distant goal. They carried with them the hopes of thousands who dreamed of freedom, and they moved forward with the knowledge that they were part of something far greater than themselves. They were a force of the oppressed, a symbol of defiance in a world ruled by power and cruelty.

Spartacus's army was no longer a band of fugitives. They were a movement, a rebellion, and for Rome, an undeniable threat that demanded a response. The next phase of the journey would test everything they had built—their unity, their resolve, and their commitment to the dream of a life beyond Rome's reach.

THE FIRST VICTORIES

With an army of freed slaves, gladiators, and those who yearned for liberation, Spartacus led his forces into the heart of Italy. What had begun as a daring escape was now an open rebellion, one that had already shocked Rome by defying their first attempts at suppression. Spartacus's army, though still rough and diverse, had tasted victory, and with each skirmish, their confidence grew. But these early victories were not just about defeating Roman forces; they were about proving to themselves—and to the world—that a coalition of the oppressed could stand against the might of an empire.

In this chapter, we will follow the army's first decisive battles, examine the strategic brilliance Spartacus displayed, and explore the morale-boosting effect these wins had on his followers. The first victories were not merely military successes; they were the foundations of a movement that would inspire fear in the hearts of Rome's elite and hope in the eyes of Rome's oppressed.

The Skirmishes in the Foothills

After breaking free from Capua and arming themselves, Spartacus and his followers took to the Italian countryside, moving from place to place to avoid Roman patrols and raid estates for supplies. The hilly terrain of southern Italy worked to their advantage. Spartacus knew how to use the landscape, setting up ambushes in narrow passes and along winding trails, where the Roman forces' strict formation and heavy armor were more of a hindrance than a help.

These small but significant victories began with ambushes on smaller Roman patrols sent to locate and suppress the rebellion. Roman soldiers, disciplined in formation fighting on open fields, found themselves at a disadvantage against Spartacus's guerrilla tactics. Spartacus's army was agile, resourceful, and driven by a desperation that gave them an edge over the professional soldiers who fought only for duty or pay. In these first battles, Spartacus's men used every advantage they could, striking swiftly and retreating before the Romans could organize a defense.

The victories in the foothills were a critical learning experience for Spartacus's soldiers, many of whom were facing trained Roman soldiers for the first time. Spartacus himself was not only a fierce fighter but also an attentive leader who adjusted his tactics based on the battlefield. After each skirmish, he and his commanders discussed what had worked and what hadn't, learning from each engagement and refining their approach.

The Battle of Vesuvius: A Stunning Defeat for Rome

One of the most remarkable of these early victories took place on the slopes of Mount Vesuvius. The Roman Senate, now fully aware of the rebellion, had dispatched a praetor named Gaius Claudius Glaber with a force of several thousand soldiers to put down Spartacus's uprising. Glaber believed that his superior numbers and discipline would easily crush the rebels, and he pursued

Spartacus to the mountainous region near Vesuvius, where he believed he had cornered the rebel force.

Confident of victory, Glaber's men set up camp at the base of Vesuvius, blocking the only visible way down. However, Spartacus had no intention of surrendering. Observing the terrain carefully, he noticed a steep, narrow path along the side of the mountain that was hidden by dense vegetation. It was a treacherous route, but Spartacus saw it as their only chance. Rallying his followers, he led them up the path, and under the cover of night, they descended behind the Roman encampment, completely unnoticed.

At dawn, Spartacus's forces launched a surprise attack on the Romans from above. The suddenness of the assault, combined with the rebels' fierce resolve, threw the Roman soldiers into disarray. Glaber's men, who had expected to starve out the rebels rather than engage in close combat, were overwhelmed. Spartacus and his followers fought with a tenacity born of desperation and hope, cutting through the Roman lines and leaving Glaber's forces in shambles.

The Battle of Vesuvius was a stunning victory, and it sent a powerful message to Rome: Spartacus was not merely a fugitive; he was a formidable leader with the tactical genius to turn even the harshest terrain to his advantage. The morale boost for Spartacus's army was immeasurable. The men who had once doubted their chances now believed they could defy Rome itself, and more enslaved people flocked to their ranks, inspired by the stories of Spartacus's triumph.

Reactions Across Italy: Fear and Inspiration

The news of Spartacus's victory at Vesuvius spread rapidly, sparking both fear and hope across Italy. For Rome's elite, this was an intolerable affront, a stain on their reputation and a threat to the social order. The idea that slaves, the very foundation of their economy, could rise up and defeat a Roman praetor was both unthinkable and terrifying. Many wealthy Romans began to worry not only about Spartacus's growing army but also about the enslaved people within their own households. They feared that Spartacus's rebellion might inspire further revolts, leading to instability across the empire.

For enslaved people, however, the victory at Vesuvius was a beacon of hope. Spartacus's name began to carry a legendary weight, a symbol of courage and defiance against impossible odds. People across the countryside, some of whom had spent years in servitude, felt the pull of freedom and began to make their way to Spartacus's camp. His army swelled with men and women who had nothing to lose, who saw in Spartacus's rebellion a chance to reclaim their lives and escape the brutality of Rome.

Consolidating Power and Gaining Resources

With a growing force, Spartacus needed more than just weapons; he needed food, supplies, and a strategy for sustaining his army. After each victory, Spartacus's forces raided nearby estates, taking provisions, equipment, and occasionally livestock. But Spartacus was careful not to engage in unnecessary cruelty or looting, as he understood that his followers viewed this rebellion as a righteous fight, not a descent into lawlessness.

Spartacus's restraint in dealing with local populations set him apart from the Roman soldiers, who were often notorious for pillaging and terrorizing the regions they entered. Instead, Spartacus encouraged his men to treat locals with respect, sometimes even offering protection to communities that supported them. This approach earned Spartacus a measure of goodwill from the Italian countryside, where resentment toward Rome simmered among the free poor and other marginalized groups who had little love for the Senate or the wealthy landowners.

In this way, Spartacus began to build not only an army but also a network of sympathizers and allies who saw his rebellion as a fight for justice against an unjust system. His tactical successes, combined with his reputation for fairness, attracted even more followers, many of whom brought their own skills and knowledge to strengthen the movement. Among his ranks were former farmers who understood the land, blacksmiths who could repair weapons, and herbalists who could treat wounds. Spartacus's army was growing not just in numbers but in capability, transforming into a self-sustaining force that could survive in the face of prolonged conflict.

The Psychological Impact on Rome

Spartacus's victories, especially at Vesuvius, had a profound psychological impact on Rome. The Senate, already concerned by the scale of the rebellion, realized that Spartacus's forces were not a mere rabble but a disciplined, strategically capable army led by a brilliant and charismatic leader. Roman politicians and generals were forced to confront the fact that their initial attempts to suppress the revolt had only strengthened Spartacus's resolve and made him a hero among the oppressed.

Rome's elite was divided on how to handle the situation. Some advocated sending larger forces to crush the rebellion decisively, while others argued for caution, fearing that a heavy-handed approach might inspire more slaves to revolt. This division slowed Rome's response, buying Spartacus precious time to solidify his army and prepare for the inevitable escalation of the conflict.

The average Roman citizen, meanwhile, viewed the rebellion with a mixture of fear and fascination. Reports of Spartacus's victories were discussed in taverns, markets, and public forums, where ordinary people speculated about the strength and purpose of this "army of slaves." Many began to view Spartacus not only as a threat but as a symbol of resistance against a system that favored the wealthy and powerful at the expense of the common people.

Strengthening the Chain of Command

As Spartacus's army grew, he recognized the need for a clear command structure. He appointed trusted lieutenants, including Crixus and Oenomaus, both of whom had proven themselves as fierce fighters and loyal followers. These commanders helped Spartacus manage the growing ranks, organize training, and enforce discipline. Spartacus also began to delegate responsibilities, relying on experienced fighters to oversee training, strategists to plan the movement of troops, and scouts to keep watch for Roman patrols.

This structure allowed Spartacus's army to function more efficiently and adapt quickly to the shifting circumstances of guerrilla warfare. Crixus, in particular, became a central figure in the army, leading his own units and developing a reputation for bravery and unrelenting ferocity on the battlefield. Though Crixus and Spartacus did not always agree on tactics or strategy, their combined efforts gave the army a unique balance of strength and adaptability.

Preparing for the Coming Storm

While Spartacus's victories brought confidence to his followers, he knew that Rome would not sit idle for long. The Senate would eventually send a formidable force, and Spartacus was well aware of the challenges that lay ahead. He used the time after each victory to regroup, train, and assess the army's resources. The goal of crossing the Alps and escaping Rome's reach still lay before them, but Spartacus was pragmatic. He knew they would have to face Rome head-on, at least for now, to secure the path to freedom.

Each victory brought its own challenges, as more followers joined the army, and more Roman forces were mobilized against them. Spartacus worked tirelessly to instill in his army not only a fighting spirit but a vision of what they were fighting for. He reminded them that they were not merely rebels or fugitives; they were men and women striving for a life free from Rome's chains. This purpose kept them moving forward, through exhaustion, injury, and loss.

The Momentum of Victory

These early victories gave Spartacus's army an unstoppable momentum. His followers no longer saw themselves as slaves or gladiators but as soldiers in a righteous cause. Each victory reaffirmed their belief in Spartacus's leadership, and the morale of the army grew with each battle they won. For the first time in their lives, many of Spartacus's followers felt a sense of purpose and dignity—a feeling that had been denied to them under Roman rule.

Spartacus's early victories were not just triumphs over Rome's soldiers; they were battles that reshaped the minds and spirits of his followers. They were a testament to the power of the oppressed, a promise that even the mightiest empire could be challenged. With each victory, Spartacus moved closer to the impossible dream he held for his people—a life beyond the Alps, a life where no one would live in chains.

Yet, Spartacus knew the storm was coming. Rome was preparing, and soon they would face an enemy more formidable than any they had encountered before. But for now, the victories were theirs, and with each one, they marched forward, defying Rome's power and embodying the spirit of freedom that no empire could ever fully crush.

DEFYING THE ROMAN LEGIONS

As Spartacus's rebellion continued to gain momentum, the Roman Senate could no longer dismiss it as a mere uprising of escaped slaves. The victories Spartacus had achieved were both an insult and a threat to the very core of Roman authority. With each defeat, the Senate's concern deepened, and they began to realize that Spartacus and his followers were not only resourceful but led by a commander of formidable skill and determination. Rome's response would soon escalate, and Spartacus's rebellion would face its most daunting challenge yet: the full might of the Roman legions.

In this chapter, we delve into the confrontations that marked Spartacus's daring stand against Rome's professional army. Spartacus's strategies, his army's resilience, and the escalating tension with Rome all played out in a series of battles that would test the limits of their courage and commitment.

Rome's Response: Underestimating Spartacus No More

Following the devastating losses at Vesuvius and other smaller skirmishes, the Roman Senate decided it was time to deal with Spartacus seriously. They realized that sending smaller detachments and local militias was no longer sufficient. The Senate feared that Spartacus's rebellion might inspire other enslaved people across Italy and the provinces to rise up, destabilizing the empire. In an attempt to crush the rebellion, the Senate authorized a campaign led by experienced military commanders, armed with the resources and men needed to take on Spartacus's forces.

The Senate assigned two consuls to lead the campaign, each with a substantial legion under their command. These legions were Rome's most disciplined and highly trained soldiers, veterans of countless campaigns. Rome believed that these elite forces would be able to subdue Spartacus and restore order. They expected a swift victory, confident that no group of former slaves, no matter how determined, could stand against the might of their professional soldiers.

Spartacus's Strategy: Outmaneuvering the Legions

Spartacus knew he was now facing the full force of the Roman army, but he was undeterred. Rather than meeting the Roman legions head-on, where their superior training and equipment would overwhelm his troops, Spartacus adopted a strategy of mobility and unpredictability. He used his knowledge of terrain, the element of surprise, and unconventional tactics to outmaneuver the Roman forces at every opportunity.

Spartacus's army, though lacking in formal military training, had two key advantages: speed and motivation. His soldiers were no longer just escapees and slaves; they had become skilled in guerrilla warfare, adept at ambushes and hit-and-run attacks. Spartacus divided his forces into smaller, mobile units, allowing them to strike quickly and then retreat before the Romans could regroup. These tactics frustrated the Roman commanders, who found it increasingly difficult to engage Spartacus's forces in open battle.

To make matters worse for the Romans, Spartacus had spies and informants scattered across the countryside who kept him informed of Roman movements. With this network, he could anticipate the Romans' plans and stay one step ahead. This intelligence proved invaluable in allowing Spartacus to evade large-scale confrontations, engaging only on his own terms and only when the terrain or circumstances gave him a distinct advantage.

The Battle of Picenum: A Shocking Upset

One of the most significant early encounters between Spartacus's army and the full might of the Roman legions took place near the town of Picenum in central Italy. The consular forces, confident in their training and numerical superiority, believed they had Spartacus's forces cornered. The Roman legions set up camp, prepared to launch a decisive attack at dawn. However, Spartacus once again employed his trademark strategy of surprise.

Using his knowledge of the landscape, Spartacus led his forces through a dense forest under the cover of night. By dawn, his soldiers had positioned themselves around the Roman encampment, hidden in the undergrowth and prepared for an ambush. When the Romans began to advance, expecting to face Spartacus in open combat, they were caught off-guard by a coordinated assault on their flanks.

The rebels attacked with precision, exploiting the Romans' lack of readiness and the disorder caused by the sudden assault. Spartacus's forces fought with an intensity and unity that surprised the consuls, who had expected to face an unruly mob rather than a disciplined force. The Roman forces fell into disarray, unable to reform their lines in the face of the relentless attacks from Spartacus's soldiers. By the end of the day, the Roman legions had suffered heavy casualties, and Spartacus's forces had emerged victorious.

The victory at Picenum was a severe blow to the Roman campaign, and it cemented Spartacus's reputation as a master strategist. News of this battle spread quickly, deepening Rome's shame and making Spartacus a hero to those who longed for freedom. The Roman Senate, humiliated by yet another defeat, was forced to rethink its strategy and prepare for an even more serious confrontation.

Spartacus's Growing Army and the Internal Divisions

The victory at Picenum brought thousands more to Spartacus's side. His army, which had started as a band of gladiators and fugitives, was now an organized force of tens of thousands. However, managing such a large group posed new challenges. With growing numbers came greater logistical demands for food, shelter, and coordination. Spartacus now commanded a population that included not only fighters but also families, elderly people, and children who had joined in pursuit of freedom.

As the army grew, so did internal divisions. Some, like Crixus, believed they should march southward and attack Rome directly, striking at the heart of their oppressor. Crixus, a bold and passionate Gaul, argued that the time had come to take the fight to the Romans, to give them a taste of the fear and suffering they had inflicted upon others. Spartacus, however, was more cautious. He believed that their best hope lay in escaping Italy altogether, ideally by crossing the Alps and finding safety in the free lands beyond Rome's reach.

These differing opinions created a rift within the ranks, and eventually, Crixus and his followers chose to break off from

Spartacus's main force. They sought glory in direct combat with the Romans, hoping to achieve a symbolic victory that would resonate across Italy. Unfortunately, this decision would have tragic consequences, as Crixus and his followers, outnumbered and lacking Spartacus's strategic support, were eventually defeated by the Romans. The loss of Crixus and his men was a painful blow to Spartacus, a reminder of the dangers posed by division and the ruthlessness of the Roman army.

The Battle of Mutina: Defying Rome's Authority

The next major confrontation occurred near Mutina, a Roman stronghold where yet another legion was stationed. Rome, humiliated by Spartacus's continued defiance, was now focused on bringing him to heel. Spartacus, however, was determined to show Rome that he was not to be underestimated. Instead of retreating, Spartacus advanced toward the Roman forces, catching them off-guard.

In a daring and meticulously planned maneuver, Spartacus and his commanders executed a multi-pronged attack on the Roman encampment. His forces, using their guerrilla tactics, approached from multiple directions, sowing confusion among the Roman soldiers. Spartacus himself led one of the main attacks, inspiring his troops with his courage and determination. As he charged forward, his followers felt as though they were fighting not just for themselves, but for the idea of freedom that Spartacus embodied.

The Romans, accustomed to fighting organized armies, struggled to respond to the unpredictable and fluid tactics of Spartacus's forces. Spartacus's soldiers, many of whom had little formal training, fought with a tenacity that the Roman soldiers could not match. The battle was fierce and brutal, but by its end, Spartacus had once again emerged victorious, leaving the Roman army devastated and humiliated.

The victory at Mutina was a turning point for Spartacus's army, marking a rare instance where they had directly confronted a full Roman legion and won. This battle sent a powerful message to the Senate, showing that Spartacus was more than just a rebel—he was a force to be reckoned with. Rome's control over its territories was slipping, and Spartacus's name had become a rallying cry for the oppressed.

The Roman Response: Summoning Crassus

The Roman Senate, desperate to end the rebellion, turned to one of Rome's wealthiest and most ambitious men: Marcus Licinius Crassus. Known for his ruthless ambition and desire for power, Crassus was given extraordinary command over multiple legions and tasked with a single mission: to crush Spartacus and his followers at any cost. Crassus accepted the challenge, seeing it as a chance to prove his military prowess and solidify his position within Roman politics.

Crassus quickly set about reorganizing his forces, imposing strict discipline and instituting brutal measures to ensure loyalty. Unlike the previous commanders, Crassus understood the gravity of the threat Spartacus posed, and he was determined not to make the same mistakes. He implemented decimation—a practice where every tenth soldier in a unit was executed—to punish any sign of cowardice or failure. This brutal discipline created a hardened, fear-driven force ready to take on Spartacus.

Spartacus, now aware of Crassus's reputation, understood that this new commander would be a formidable opponent. Crassus's arrival signaled the beginning of a new phase in the rebellion, one in which Spartacus and his followers would face not only Rome's most disciplined soldiers but also a commander who would stop at nothing to achieve victory.

The Dream of Freedom Beyond the Alps

Despite the mounting pressure from Crassus, Spartacus held to his original vision: crossing the Alps and escaping Roman territory. He understood that his army, despite its victories, could not sustain a prolonged war against the full might of Rome. He urged his followers to seize this opportunity to flee while they still had the strength and numbers to do so.

Yet many of Spartacus's followers, emboldened by their recent victories, were reluctant to leave Italy. They saw themselves as warriors, and some even harbored dreams of defeating Rome itself. Spartacus's appeals for caution were met with resistance, as the lure of revenge and the desire for freedom within Rome's borders pulled his followers in conflicting directions. It was a bitter irony: the very successes that had given them hope also made it harder for them to walk away.

The Gathering Storm

The battles with the Roman legions had tested Spartacus's army like never before, pushing them to new heights of discipline, courage, and resilience. Each victory solidified Spartacus's place as a leader and symbol of defiance. His army had transformed from a desperate band of fugitives into a force that had stood up to Rome's legions and triumphed. But Spartacus knew that the road ahead was fraught with peril. Crassus was coming, and with him, the full wrath of Rome.

The victories they had won, though sweet, had come at a cost. They had lost comrades, faced internal divisions, and drawn the attention of Rome's most ruthless general. The next phase of their journey would be the most challenging yet, as they prepared to face Crassus's legions in a confrontation that would determine the fate of the rebellion.

For Spartacus and his followers, the stakes had never been higher. They marched forward, knowing that each step brought them closer to freedom—or to a battle that would echo through history. The dream of freedom still lay before them, shimmering like a mirage, urging them onward into the unknown.

A DREAM OF FREEDOM

With each victory against the Roman forces, Spartacus's army moved one step closer to the possibility of freedom. The original vision that had driven Spartacus since his escape from Capua—the dream of leading his followers across the Alps to freedom—had kept his army united and hopeful, even in the face of unimaginable hardship. For Spartacus, the Alps represented a barrier between oppression and liberation, a natural line that separated the world of Rome from the lands beyond its reach. To cross the Alps was to finally break free from Rome's grasp, to live beyond the shadow of the empire.

However, as the rebellion grew, so did the ambitions and desires of his followers. The army had transformed from a band of fugitives into a powerful force capable of facing the Roman legions, and with this newfound strength came a hunger for something more than just escape. For some, the Alps seemed like a distant, almost unnecessary goal. Italy itself had become a battleground, and the opportunity to strike at Rome's heart, to make the oppressors feel the fear and pain they had inflicted on others, was tantalizing.

In this chapter, we explore the growing tension between Spartacus's vision of freedom beyond the Alps and the rising ambition among his followers to confront Rome directly. The Alps, so close yet so far, became a symbol of division within the army—a beacon of hope for some, and a point of contention for others.

The Alps: The Promise of Escape

Spartacus's desire to cross the Alps was rooted in his understanding of Rome's military power. He knew that as long as they remained within Roman territory, his army would be hunted. Rome's resources were vast, and the Senate would stop at nothing to end the rebellion. To Spartacus, the Alps were the only true escape, the only path that could ensure long-term safety for himself and his followers. He saw beyond the glory of battles won; he saw the harsh reality of Rome's determination and the need for a lasting solution.

In his mind, the ultimate victory lay not in defeating every Roman legion sent after them but in securing a life where Rome could no longer touch them. The freedom he envisioned was not just a temporary respite but a permanent release from the chains that had bound them. Crossing the Alps represented that future—a life of dignity and peace, where his followers could rebuild their lives, free from the relentless pursuit of Rome.

Spartacus shared this vision with his army, urging them to see the larger picture. His speeches spoke of the lands beyond the Alps, of places where they could live without fear, where the long arm of Rome could not reach. To many of his followers, particularly those who had known only the harsh life of slavery, this vision was deeply appealing. The idea of a world beyond the grasp of the empire ignited their imaginations and gave them something real to hope for.

Rising Ambition: The Call to Strike at Rome

Despite Spartacus's insistence on the goal of freedom beyond the Alps, a significant portion of his army began to see Italy itself as a new home. Emboldened by their victories, many among his ranks felt that they could continue to fight, perhaps even overthrowing Roman rule in certain regions. For the first time, the army felt like it had the power to directly challenge the state that had oppressed them.

Leaders like Crixus, a passionate and headstrong Gaul, argued that they should march southward and confront Rome. Crixus believed that retreating over the Alps would be an abandonment of their momentum, a retreat that failed to capitalize on the opportunity to strike a meaningful blow against Rome. He wanted to see Italy, the very heartland of the empire, shake with the fear that Rome had instilled in so many others. This perspective resonated with some of the more battle-hardened members of the army, particularly those who sought revenge for the years of cruelty and exploitation they had endured.

Crixus's call for a southern campaign introduced a rift within the army, dividing Spartacus's followers into two camps: those who wanted to escape and those who wanted to confront Rome head-on. The division was not just about tactics; it reflected deeper questions about the purpose of the rebellion and the nature of freedom itself. Was freedom simply escape from Rome, or did it require challenging Rome's power within Italy? For many, the idea of retreating over the Alps felt like running away, a forfeiture of the power they had fought so hard to attain.

The Emotional Pull of Revenge

For countless members of Spartacus's army, their years in bondage had been defined by brutality, injustice, and loss. The scars they bore, both physical and emotional, fueled a burning desire for revenge. They wanted Rome to feel the pain they had endured, to understand the suffering they had inflicted. The victories Spartacus's army had achieved had awakened this desire, making it hard to simply walk away.

For these men and women, freedom was not just a physical escape but an emotional reckoning. They wanted to strike fear into the hearts of the Romans, to make them understand that those they had enslaved were not mere possessions but people with strength and dignity. To cross the Alps felt, in a way, like leaving the job unfinished. Revenge, for them, was intertwined with the concept of freedom. They believed that true liberation would only come when Rome itself had been humbled.

Spartacus understood this feeling, as he himself had suffered under Roman chains. Yet he remained focused on the goal of escape. He knew that his army, for all its courage, was still vastly outnumbered and out-resourced by Rome. Every victory brought them closer to freedom, but it also made Rome's retaliation more inevitable and more severe. He respected the desire for vengeance but tried to temper it with a sense of caution and pragmatism. He reminded his followers that their lives and the lives of their families were more valuable than any momentary satisfaction of revenge.

The Decision Point: To Cross or Not to Cross

As winter approached, Spartacus and his army moved closer to the northern regions of Italy, where the Alps loomed in the distance. It was a moment of reckoning for the army, a decision point that would shape the future of the rebellion. Many of his followers stood by Spartacus's vision, eager to cross the mountains and escape Rome's grasp. The Alps represented a tangible end to their journey, a final obstacle to overcome before they could live in peace.

However, others in the army, emboldened by their victories, felt that crossing the Alps was a retreat that ignored the power they had gained. They argued that by staying in Italy, they could carve out a territory for themselves, perhaps even creating a free enclave within Roman territory. This idea of establishing a "free land" resonated with those who had come to see Italy as their home, even if it was a home drenched in blood and suffering.

Spartacus was torn. He had always held the vision of crossing the Alps, but he also felt the weight of his followers' desires and expectations. He knew that many of them would be reluctant to abandon Italy, especially after they had fought so hard to make a place for themselves. Yet he also understood that staying in Italy would mean endless warfare, a constant struggle for survival against an empire that would never cease hunting them.

The First Detour: A Move Southward

In the end, Spartacus decided to delay the crossing, opting to lead his forces southward. This decision was a compromise, a way to buy time while allowing his followers to vent their frustrations and achieve some measure of retribution. They would raid Roman estates, disrupt trade routes, and continue to build their forces as they moved. Spartacus hoped that this southward campaign would satisfy those who sought revenge, allowing the army to rally around a unified goal before making the final push for freedom.

As they marched southward, Spartacus's forces continued to grow. Enslaved people from all over Italy heard of his victories and flocked to his banner. The army became a moving symbol of defiance, a force that embodied the hope of the oppressed. They raided Roman estates, liberating those held in bondage and distributing wealth and provisions among their ranks. Spartacus's followers felt, for the first time, the sense of power and agency that had been denied to them under Roman rule.

However, this detour also had consequences. It signaled to Rome that Spartacus might be seeking a more permanent presence in Italy, perhaps even an open challenge to Roman authority. The Senate, realizing that Spartacus was not simply fleeing but actively defying their rule, intensified their efforts to eliminate him. Rome's patience was wearing thin, and they would soon turn to the most ruthless means available to end the rebellion.

The Price of Delay

While the southward campaign allowed Spartacus's army to consolidate and grow, it also allowed Rome to prepare. The delay gave Crassus, who had been appointed as the supreme commander to end the rebellion, time to organize his forces and devise a strategy. Crassus was a man of immense wealth and ambition, and he was determined to succeed where other commanders had failed. He viewed Spartacus as not only a military threat but also a political opportunity—a chance to prove his prowess and secure his place in Roman politics.

Crassus implemented harsh measures to strengthen his army's resolve, instilling a level of discipline that would prove difficult for Spartacus's forces to overcome. He ordered decimation for units that retreated or showed cowardice, sacrificing every tenth soldier in a brutal display of authority. Crassus's approach was ruthless, but it ensured that his army would fight with unrelenting determination. Spartacus, watching Crassus's tactics from a distance, understood that he was now facing a more dangerous opponent than ever before.

Reigniting the Vision of Freedom

As Crassus's forces drew closer, Spartacus returned to his original goal, urging his followers to focus once again on the dream of freedom beyond the Alps. He reminded them that their ultimate purpose was not to conquer Rome or seek revenge but to live freely. He knew that Crassus would bring everything he had to the fight, and Spartacus did not want his followers to die in a futile battle when they still had a chance at true freedom.

With winter approaching, Spartacus prepared to lead his forces northward once again. The path was perilous, and the mountains were a formidable obstacle, but Spartacus was determined to pursue his vision. His speeches reignited the hope that had brought his army together in the first place, a reminder that they were fighting for a life beyond the brutality of Rome.

A Path Not Taken

The decision to move southward, though tactically sound in some respects, ultimately delayed Spartacus's escape. It intensified Rome's determination to crush the rebellion and brought Crassus's full force to bear against them. The dream of freedom still loomed on the other side of the Alps, tantalizingly close yet further than ever.

Spartacus and his followers continued to march, their hopes undimmed but their path increasingly fraught with peril. They had defied Rome, inspired countless others, and held onto their dream of freedom against impossible odds. But now, as they turned once again toward the north, they would face their greatest and most dangerous challenge yet.

The mountains were calling, but so was Rome's vengeance. The path to freedom was narrowing, and Spartacus knew that their final stand was drawing near.

THE BRUTAL ENDGAME

As Spartacus led his army northward once again, the looming presence of Rome grew ever closer. Marcus Licinius Crassus, the Senate's appointed commander, was no ordinary opponent. He was wealthy, ambitious, and ruthlessly efficient, willing to do whatever it took to crush the rebellion once and for all. Crassus's arrival marked the beginning of a merciless campaign, an all-out assault on Spartacus and his followers that would culminate in a series of bloody, unrelenting confrontations.

This chapter delves into the final phase of the rebellion, a desperate struggle where hope, courage, and survival collided with the relentless power of Rome. It explores Crassus's brutal tactics, Spartacus's attempts to evade and outmaneuver him, and the courage of those who followed Spartacus to the bitter end.

Crassus's Strategy: Brutal Discipline and Relentless Pursuit

Crassus was a man of wealth and influence, but more than anything, he was driven by a thirst for power and recognition.

His command over the campaign against Spartacus was not merely a military duty; it was an opportunity to demonstrate his capabilities and secure his place within Roman politics. Unlike the previous Roman commanders who had underestimated Spartacus, Crassus understood the gravity of the threat. He knew that Spartacus was no ordinary opponent and that defeating him would require a relentless, uncompromising strategy.

To instill discipline and obedience among his troops, Crassus revived the ancient and brutal punishment of decimation. When a unit showed cowardice or failed to perform as expected, Crassus ordered every tenth soldier to be executed by their own comrades. This brutal punishment instilled fear within his ranks, ensuring that no soldier would dare retreat or falter in the face of Spartacus's forces. Crassus's army became a fear-driven machine, ready to fight without hesitation and with unwavering loyalty to their commander.

Crassus also implemented a strategy of relentless pursuit, refusing to allow Spartacus's army any chance to rest or regroup. He divided his forces to create a blockade, cutting off potential escape routes and driving Spartacus's army toward a cornered position. Crassus was determined to exhaust the rebels, forcing them into a confrontation that would end the rebellion once and for all.

Spartacus's Attempts at Diplomacy and Escape

As Crassus's forces closed in, Spartacus understood that his options were dwindling. He faced a relentless enemy who would not stop until his army was destroyed. Knowing the danger they were in, Spartacus explored every possible alternative, including diplomacy. In a last attempt to avoid a final, devastating battle, Spartacus tried to negotiate passage with pirate groups on the

Italian coast, hoping to secure ships that could transport his people out of Italy. He hoped that, by reaching Sicily or other distant lands, his followers could escape Rome's grasp and rebuild their lives in peace.

However, the deal fell through. The pirates, after initially agreeing to transport Spartacus's army, ultimately betrayed him, taking payment and abandoning him and his followers without a way to escape by sea. This betrayal was a devastating setback, stripping Spartacus's forces of one of their last viable options for escape. With no ships and no route out, Spartacus knew that they were now trapped within Italy, forced to face the Roman legions head-on.

Despite this, Spartacus did not lose hope. He continued to inspire his followers, urging them to stay together and reminding them of the life they were fighting for. Though their path to freedom had been cut off, he believed that they could still survive, that they could still defy Rome to the end. His unwavering courage, even in the face of impossible odds, rallied his followers, many of whom were willing to die rather than surrender.

The Final Stand: The Battle on the Silarus River

As Crassus tightened his grip on the rebels, he finally succeeded in cornering Spartacus's forces near the Silarus River in southern Italy. Crassus's strategy had worked; Spartacus's army, exhausted and out of options, had nowhere left to go. The rebels found themselves facing a Roman force that outnumbered them, equipped with superior weaponry and discipline. For Spartacus, this was the ultimate test of his leadership and courage.

In the days leading up to the final battle, Spartacus made a fateful decision. He gathered his closest followers, inspiring them with one last, passionate speech. He reminded them that they were fighting for their dignity, for their freedom, and for a life beyond the tyranny of Rome. He encouraged those who wished to escape to do so, knowing that they faced almost certain death. But for many, the thought of deserting Spartacus was unthinkable. They had come too far, fought too many battles, and sacrificed too much to abandon their leader now. Spartacus's courage had been the guiding force of the rebellion, and his followers were determined to stand by him to the end.

On the morning of the battle, Spartacus symbolically mounted a horse, preparing to lead his men into combat one last time. But before charging into battle, he is said to have slain his horse—a final act symbolizing his commitment to stand with his followers, to live or die with them rather than attempting to escape. Spartacus, even in this darkest hour, displayed the same unwavering bravery that had inspired thousands to follow him.

The Clash: Courage Against Impossible Odds

The Battle of the Silarus River was brutal and bloody. Crassus's legions, driven by discipline and a ruthless commitment to victory, advanced with relentless precision, pushing Spartacus's forces back with each wave. Spartacus's army fought with desperate courage, knowing that this was their last stand. They fought not only for survival but for the ideals of freedom and dignity that had defined their journey.

Despite being outnumbered and exhausted, Spartacus's forces fought valiantly. Using every tactic they had learned, every ounce of strength left in their bodies, they resisted the Roman advance, refusing to surrender even as the odds mounted against them. Spartacus himself fought at the front lines, wielding his weapon with the same skill and ferocity that had made him a feared gladiator. He was a leader in battle as much as he was in spirit, rallying his men and urging them forward even as the Romans closed in around them.

The battlefield was a chaotic, deadly arena, where courage and desperation collided with the brutal efficiency of Rome's military. The ground became a sea of bodies as the rebel forces were steadily overwhelmed by the sheer numbers and discipline of the Roman legions. But Spartacus's followers did not retreat. They fought to the last, driven by loyalty to their leader and the hope that, in death, they would find a freedom that Rome could never take from them.

The Death of Spartacus: A Symbolic End

According to historical accounts, Spartacus was killed in the heat of battle, surrounded by his enemies. His body was never found, lost among the thousands who had died that day. His death marked the end of the rebellion, but his legacy was already immortalized. Spartacus had defied the mightiest empire of his time, leading a movement that inspired thousands and terrified the Roman elite. Though Rome had crushed the rebellion, they could not erase the memory of Spartacus, the gladiator who became a symbol of resistance.

With Spartacus's death, Crassus ordered the crucifixion of thousands of captured rebels along the Appian Way, the road leading from Rome to Capua. The sight was meant as a warning to others who might dare to challenge Rome. The bodies of Spartacus's followers lined the road for miles, a brutal reminder of Rome's power and the cost of defying it. But to many, these men were not merely criminals—they were martyrs, people who had fought for a chance at freedom and died rather than return to a life of servitude.

The Legacy of Spartacus

The rebellion may have been crushed, but Spartacus's spirit

endured. His life and his struggle became a source of inspiration for generations to come. To the oppressed, the marginalized, and those who lived under tyranny, Spartacus was a hero, a symbol of courage and the unyielding human desire for freedom. His name echoed through history, a reminder that even the greatest empires could be challenged by the resilience of those they had oppressed.

Spartacus's legacy extended beyond the battlefield, influencing later revolts and inspiring countless movements that sought justice and equality. His story became a testament to the strength of the human spirit, an enduring reminder that even in the face of impossible odds, the fight for freedom is never in vain.

In the years that followed, Rome would continue to face challenges and unrest, but the memory of Spartacus remained. He had shown the world that a slave, a gladiator, a man from the fringes of society, could become a beacon of resistance. His rebellion may have ended in blood and crucifixion, but his ideals lived on, carried by those who refused to accept the shackles of oppression.

The Price of Freedom

The brutal end of Spartacus's rebellion underscored the heavy price of defying Rome, but it also revealed the power of hope, courage, and unity in the face of oppression. Spartacus's dream of freedom had inspired thousands to rise up, to fight for a life of dignity, even if it meant facing death. His death did not diminish the strength of his ideals; if anything, it immortalized them.

Rome's victory may have restored order, but the empire could never silence the story of Spartacus. His rebellion, though ultimately unsuccessful in its immediate goals, left a profound legacy that would resonate across time. Spartacus's life, his courage, and his commitment to freedom became an inspiration for all who would follow, a reminder that even the most powerful empires are not invincible.

THE LAST STAND

As the rebellion neared its end, Spartacus and his remaining followers faced a grim reality. They had defied Rome for nearly two years, achieving victories that stunned the empire and inspired hope in countless oppressed people. But with each victory, Rome's resolve had only grown stronger, culminating in Crassus's ruthless campaign to crush them once and for all. Now cornered, outnumbered, and exhausted, Spartacus prepared for a final, defiant stand against the forces of Rome.

In this chapter, we explore the tense days leading up to the last battle, the decisions Spartacus made, and the emotional strength of his followers as they faced almost certain death. The last stand of Spartacus was not only a physical confrontation but a symbolic end to one of the most significant rebellions of ancient history.

The Morale of a Doomed Army

By the time Spartacus's forces faced Crassus's legions at the Silarus River, they were worn down, having survived numerous battles and a relentless pursuit across Italy. Their numbers had dwindled, and supplies were scarce. For weeks, they had been pushed further south, hemmed in by Crassus's legions and with no path to escape. But despite the looming threat of death, Spartacus's followers remained committed to their leader and to each other. Many were bound not just by a desire for freedom, but by a sense of loyalty and unity forged through hardship.

Spartacus's followers knew that they had little chance of winning the final battle, yet they remained steadfast. They had come to accept that their rebellion might end in blood, but they also understood that their struggle had proven something powerful—that those who were enslaved and oppressed could rise against the mightiest empire of their time. Each follower felt that they had a role in this symbolic stand, that their defiance alone would leave a mark on history.

Spartacus himself moved through the camp in those final days, speaking with his followers, rallying their spirits, and sharing moments of solidarity. He spoke not of escape or retreat, but of the courage that had brought them this far. He reminded them that they were not just soldiers or slaves, but people who had reclaimed their dignity and chosen to live and die on their own terms. Spartacus's words strengthened their resolve, imbuing them with a sense of purpose that transcended mere survival.

Spartacus's Final Strategy

Though he knew that victory was nearly impossible, Spartacus was determined to fight with all the skill and cunning he had developed throughout the rebellion. His plan was to divide Crassus's forces by launching an aggressive charge, aiming to break through the Roman lines in a desperate attempt to create an escape route. Spartacus believed that if they could disrupt the disciplined ranks of Crassus's army, they might find a chance to escape the encirclement or at least buy themselves time.

Spartacus prepared his men for the battle, organizing them into units and assigning roles based on their individual strengths. Those who had been trained as gladiators would lead the charge, using their close-combat skills to engage the Roman front lines. Spartacus placed his most experienced fighters in key positions, hoping to maximize their impact in the first moments of the attack.

He made a symbolic gesture before the battle, reportedly slaying his own horse to demonstrate that he would stand and fight alongside his men, with no intention of fleeing. By killing his horse, Spartacus sent a clear message to his followers: he would face the same fate as they would, whether that meant victory or death. The sight of their leader dismounting and pledging to stand with them moved his followers deeply, cementing their loyalty to him in their final hours.

The Battle Begins: A Charge of Defiance

At dawn, the rebels launched their final charge, with Spartacus at the forefront. The sight of Spartacus, armed and leading his followers directly into the heart of the Roman legions, was a powerful image—one that would be etched into the memories of those who witnessed it. The rebels, outnumbered and poorly armed compared to the disciplined legions, advanced with a courage born of desperation and loyalty to their leader.

The initial impact of the charge was intense, as Spartacus's forces clashed with the Roman soldiers in brutal hand-to-hand combat. The rebels fought with everything they had, displaying a ferocity that surprised even Crassus's hardened troops. Despite their lack of armor and superior weaponry, Spartacus's men used every technique they knew, employing a combination of gladiatorial skills and guerrilla tactics to hold their ground.

Spartacus himself was a force on the battlefield, wielding his weapon with deadly precision and inspiring his followers to push forward. Those who fought beside him saw the same strength and courage that had led them to defy Rome in the first place. Spartacus moved through the ranks of his enemies, cutting down soldiers and rallying his men, determined to break through the Roman lines.

The Roman Counterattack

Crassus, however, had anticipated Spartacus's move. He was prepared for the charge and had positioned his forces to absorb the impact. The Roman legions, disciplined and fortified by years of training, held their lines under the assault, slowly wearing down Spartacus's forces. The legions began to close in, surrounding the rebels on all sides and forcing them into a tight, confined space. As the Roman soldiers pressed forward, the advantage shifted increasingly in their favor.

Crassus's forces executed their tactics with ruthless precision, gradually breaking the rebels' formations and inflicting devastating losses. The rebels fought with desperate bravery, refusing to surrender, but they were overwhelmed by the sheer numbers and discipline of the Roman legions. Spartacus's dream of breaking through the lines and escaping grew fainter with each passing moment as the Romans closed their trap.

Spartacus's Last Moments

Accounts of Spartacus's final moments vary, but historians generally agree that he fought to the very end, refusing to surrender or retreat. Surrounded by Roman soldiers, Spartacus continued to fight, cutting down enemy after enemy in a desperate attempt to keep his followers safe. His courage and tenacity in those final moments became legendary, as he demonstrated the same defiance that had defined his life and rebellion.

As the battle reached its climax, Spartacus was eventually overpowered. His body was never definitively identified among the fallen, adding a sense of mystery to his final stand. To his followers, Spartacus's death was both a loss and a profound symbol of resistance. He had chosen to die in battle rather than submit to Roman rule, embodying the very ideals of freedom and courage that had driven the rebellion from the beginning.

Even as the Roman soldiers swarmed over the battlefield, searching for any remnants of the rebel force, Spartacus's memory endured. For his followers and for future generations, Spartacus became an icon of defiance, a leader who had dared to challenge the might of Rome and had died rather than submit. His final moments on the battlefield were a testament to the strength of the human spirit and the power of a dream that could not be extinguished, even in death.

The Aftermath: A Grim Message from Rome

With Spartacus dead and the rebellion crushed, Crassus ordered the brutal punishment of the surviving rebels. He lined the Appian Way with the bodies of thousands of captured rebels, crucifying them as a warning to anyone who might consider challenging Rome. The sight was a grim reminder of Rome's power and cruelty, a stark display of the consequences of defiance. For miles, the roads were lined with the bodies of men who had once fought for freedom, a visual testament to the empire's unyielding authority.

To Rome, the brutal display was meant to restore order and discourage further rebellion. But to others, it became a rallying cry, a symbol of the courage and resilience of those who had dared to fight. Though Spartacus and his rebellion had been defeated, their ideals lived on, inspiring generations to come.

Spartacus's Legacy

Though he had fallen in battle, Spartacus's legacy endured, shaping history and inspiring movements of resistance for centuries. He became a symbol of defiance against oppression, a reminder that even the mightiest empires could be challenged. To those who suffered under the rule of Rome and other tyrannies throughout history, Spartacus represented the possibility of rebellion, the hope that even the most marginalized could rise up and demand freedom.

The story of Spartacus spread far beyond Rome, carried through the years by writers, historians, and storytellers who saw in his life a story worth preserving. To this day, Spartacus remains a symbol of courage and resilience, a figure who embodies the universal struggle for freedom and dignity. His life, his rebellion, and his final stand have inspired countless individuals, movements, and causes that sought to challenge oppression and reclaim human dignity.

The Eternal Flame of Defiance

The last stand of Spartacus was a defining moment, not just for his followers, but for history itself. Though his rebellion ended in blood and death, his legacy proved indomitable. Spartacus's life was a testament to the strength of the human spirit, a reminder that even in the face of overwhelming power, the fight for freedom is never in vain.

Rome had won the battle, but it could not erase the memory of Spartacus and his followers. The ideals they fought for lived on, inspiring future generations to challenge injustice, to resist oppression, and to believe in the power of courage and unity.

Spartacus's last stand was more than a battle—it was a declaration, a statement of hope, and a flame that continues to burn through history.

Though he died on the battlefield, Spartacus achieved a form of immortality. He remains a hero to those who believe in freedom, a legend that endures as long as there are those willing to stand against tyranny. In the end, the true victory of Spartacus was not in the battles he won but in the legacy of defiance he left behind.

SPARTACUS'S LEGACY

Though Spartacus's rebellion ended in defeat, his story did not end on the blood-soaked fields of Italy. The life and actions of Spartacus, the gladiator-turned-rebel who defied the most powerful empire of his time, resonated far beyond his death, becoming a powerful symbol of resistance and an inspiration to countless generations. His legacy transformed him from a mere historical figure into a legend—a timeless icon of courage, freedom, and defiance against oppression.

In this chapter, we examine the impact Spartacus had on history and the enduring power of his legacy. From the years following his rebellion to the modern era, Spartacus's story has continued to inspire those who seek justice and liberation. His legacy serves as a reminder that even in the face of insurmountable odds, one person's stand for freedom can inspire movements that change the course of history.

Rome's Fear of Future Revolts

In the immediate aftermath of Spartacus's rebellion, Rome was left shaken. The rebellion had exposed vulnerabilities in the empire's control over its vast enslaved population. For the first time, Rome's rulers saw the potential threat that lay within their own borders—a threat that could undermine the very foundation of their society. Spartacus's rebellion revealed that enslaved people, when united under a capable leader, could challenge the Roman legions themselves.

To prevent further uprisings, the Senate enacted stricter laws governing enslaved people, increasing surveillance, and implementing harsher punishments for any sign of dissent. The legacy of Spartacus's rebellion led to intensified repression, as Rome sought to crush any spark of defiance before it could ignite. Crassus's brutal execution of Spartacus's captured followers along the Appian Way was not only a punishment but a calculated act of deterrence, a visual warning to those who might dare to rebel.

Yet, despite these efforts, Spartacus's legacy could not be erased. The memory of his rebellion remained embedded in the collective consciousness of the oppressed, inspiring quiet acts of resistance and instilling in enslaved people a sense of possibility. Spartacus's legacy lived on as a hidden, simmering threat within Rome, a reminder to the empire that the desire for freedom could not be silenced, even by the strongest of chains.

Spartacus in Historical Memory

In the years following his death, Spartacus was remembered in various ways by historians, writers, and the general public. Roman historians, often writing from the perspective of the elite, portrayed him as a dangerous outlaw, a criminal who had dared to defy the state. However, they also acknowledged his skill, his charisma, and his ability to command loyalty.

Some, like the historian Plutarch, recognized Spartacus's unique qualities, noting his intelligence, nobility, and commitment to his followers. These accounts, while biased, preserved Spartacus's story, ensuring that his legacy would survive through history.

As time passed, Spartacus became a figure of fascination for writers and thinkers across different cultures. In medieval Europe, his story re-emerged in folklore as tales of heroic rebels and champions of justice spread through oral traditions. Though distorted by time and interpretation, the core of Spartacus's legacy remained intact: he was a leader who had fought for freedom, a man who had refused to submit to tyranny.

By the Enlightenment period, thinkers and writers who advocated for justice and human rights began to draw on Spartacus's story as an example of defiance against oppression. He was viewed as a hero for those who believed in equality and liberty, and his story was cited as evidence that the desire for freedom was an innate human impulse, present across time and cultures.

Spartacus as a Symbol in Modern Revolutions

The legacy of Spartacus reached a new level of prominence in the 18th and 19th centuries, during a time of global revolutions and social upheaval. As movements for freedom and equality spread, Spartacus became a symbol for those who sought to challenge authoritarian rule. Revolutionary leaders and thinkers saw in Spartacus a model of courage and defiance, a figure who embodied the struggle against oppression and the fight for human dignity.

During the French Revolution, Spartacus's name was evoked by leaders who saw themselves as champions of the oppressed. He was held up as an example of a leader who had stood up against the powerful and fought for the freedom of the enslaved. For the revolutionaries, Spartacus represented the idea that those at the bottom of society could rise up and demand justice, even against seemingly invincible authorities.

In the 19th century, Spartacus's legacy influenced socialist and labor movements. Karl Marx and Friedrich Engels saw him as a figure of historical significance, a precursor to their vision of class struggle and the fight against economic oppression. Marx himself described Spartacus as "the most splendid fellow in the whole of ancient history," praising his dedication to the cause of liberation. For socialist thinkers, Spartacus symbolized the unity and strength that could arise among the oppressed when they stood together.

Spartacus's influence extended to the Americas, where enslaved people and abolitionists drew inspiration from his story. Leaders of slave rebellions, like Nat Turner in the United States and Toussaint Louverture in Haiti, invoked Spartacus's legacy as they led uprisings against their oppressors. Spartacus's rebellion became a source of hope for those who longed for freedom and a powerful reminder that the struggle for human rights had deep historical roots.

Spartacus in Literature, Film, and Popular Culture

In the 20th century, Spartacus's story was immortalized through literature, film, and popular culture, reaching audiences around the world. In 1951, the novel Spartacus by Howard Fast was published, painting a sympathetic portrait of Spartacus as a leader of the oppressed. The novel was written during a period of social and political upheaval in the United States, reflecting themes of resistance against exploitation and the fight for justice. Fast's novel became immensely popular and introduced Spartacus to a new generation of readers who saw him as a timeless symbol of courage.

In 1960, Stanley Kubrick's epic film Spartacus, starring Kirk Douglas, brought Spartacus's story to the big screen. The film depicted Spartacus as a heroic figure, a man who stood against the brutal injustices of Rome, and it resonated deeply with audiences. The famous scene in which Spartacus's followers, when asked to identify him, each stand up and declare, "I am Spartacus!" became iconic, symbolizing the unity and resilience of the oppressed. The film's impact was profound, and it cemented Spartacus's place in popular culture as a symbol of defiance and human dignity.

Spartacus's story continued to inspire artistic works and media, including television series, novels, and plays. His legacy found a place in music, with bands and musicians using his name as a symbol of rebellion. Spartacus's image evolved with each retelling, but the core of his story remained unchanged: he was a man who had chosen to fight for freedom, and that choice made him a hero to all who longed for justice.

Spartacus as a Timeless Symbol of Resistance

Today, Spartacus stands as a universal symbol of the fight for freedom. His story has transcended history, inspiring movements and individuals across cultures, languages, and centuries. He is remembered as the gladiator who became a leader, the slave who became a warrior, and the man who challenged the might of an empire for the sake of dignity and liberty. Spartacus's legacy reminds us that the desire for freedom is a fundamental part of human nature, an impulse that cannot be extinguished, no matter how powerful the oppressor.

The name Spartacus has become synonymous with courage, resilience, and the power of unity. His story has inspired activists, political movements, and individuals who continue to seek justice in the face of adversity. Spartacus's rebellion serves as a reminder that history's most powerful figures are not always kings or emperors, but those who, despite overwhelming odds, stand up for the right to live free.

The Legacy of Spartacus: Lessons for the Modern World

In a world still marked by inequality, exploitation, and authoritarianism, Spartacus's story remains as relevant as ever. His life and rebellion offer valuable lessons about the importance of unity, the strength of the human spirit, and the need for courage in the pursuit of justice. Spartacus's legacy challenges us to confront oppression wherever it exists and to stand in solidarity with those who are denied their basic rights.

Spartacus reminds us that the fight for freedom is often long and fraught with sacrifice, but that it is a struggle worth undertaking. His life serves as a testament to the power of individual courage to inspire collective action, to the strength that can be found in unity, and to the resilience of those who refuse to be broken by injustice. Spartacus's legacy continues to resonate with all who believe in human dignity, and his story remains a beacon of hope for those who refuse to accept a life in chains.

The Unyielding Flame of Spartacus

Spartacus's legacy has endured through centuries, transcending his life and even his death. His story is more than a historical account; it is a call to action, a reminder that freedom is a right worth fighting for, even against impossible odds. Spartacus's life embodied the idea that no person should be forced to live in servitude, that every human being has an inherent right to dignity, and that the pursuit of freedom is a universal cause.

Though his rebellion ended on a battlefield, Spartacus achieved a form of immortality. His legacy, his courage, and his dream of a life beyond the chains have continued to inspire and empower countless individuals throughout history. Spartacus's flame—his unyielding fight for justice—remains alive, a symbol of hope that endures wherever there are those willing to resist oppression.

In the end, Spartacus's true victory lies not in the battles he fought, but in the enduring spirit of freedom he has passed on to the generations that followed. His legacy is a testament to the strength of the human soul, a reminder that even in the darkest of times, the desire for freedom can light the way forward. Spartacus's name lives on, a flame that will continue to burn as long as there are people willing to stand up and declare, "I am Spartacus."

THE ETERNAL FLAME OF REBELLION

Spartacus's story is one of the most enduring tales of resistance and hope in human history. From his life as a Thracian warrior to his transformation into a gladiator and ultimately a leader of the oppressed, Spartacus embodied a universal longing for freedom that resonates across time and cultures. Though he was defeated on the battlefield, his legacy has transcended centuries, inspiring movements, individuals, and causes dedicated to justice, equality, and human dignity.

The story of Spartacus reminds us that freedom is a powerful force, one that cannot be easily suppressed, even by the most powerful empires. His rebellion challenged the foundations of Rome itself, revealing the potential strength of those who dared to dream beyond their circumstances. Spartacus's journey from slavery to defiance, and from rebellion to legend, speaks to the unbreakable spirit within each individual who yearns for a life without chains.

The Timeless Lesson of Spartacus

The life of Spartacus teaches us that no one is born to be subjugated. His journey reflects the transformative power of courage, the strength that comes from unity, and the profound impact of a leader who truly believes in his people. Spartacus's refusal to accept a life of bondage, his willingness to fight for his followers, and his unyielding vision of freedom left an indelible mark on history, one that extends far beyond the rebellion itself.

Throughout his journey, Spartacus became more than a leader; he became a symbol of hope for those who sought to rise above their circumstances. His example challenges us to consider our own role in the fight for justice, to ask ourselves what we are willing to stand for, and to reflect on the power of one person's courage to ignite a movement. Spartacus's legacy is a call to each of us, a reminder that the pursuit of justice is a journey worth undertaking, even if it comes with sacrifice.

The Legacy of Spartacus in the Modern World

In a world that continues to grapple with issues of inequality, oppression, and injustice, Spartacus's story remains profoundly relevant. His life serves as an enduring testament to the resilience of the human spirit and the unbreakable will of those who seek a life free from tyranny. Spartacus's story reminds us that even in the face of overwhelming power, it is possible to stand for what is right, to fight for dignity, and to inspire others to do the same.

Spartacus's legacy encourages us to seek change, to recognize the strength that lies in unity, and to confront systems that deny individuals their humanity. His story is an invitation to remember the power of collective action, to believe in the possibility of a better world, and to recognize that freedom is a right that belongs to all people, regardless of their circumstances.

A Beacon of Hope and Defiance

Though centuries have passed since Spartacus walked the earth, his name remains a beacon of hope and defiance. His legacy is not confined to the pages of history but lives on in every act of resistance against injustice. From the movements for civil rights to the struggles for independence and human rights around the world, Spartacus's spirit endures, inspiring those who refuse to accept a life of oppression. His story is a reminder that the fight for freedom is not limited by time, that each generation can draw strength from the courage of those who came before.

Spartacus's rebellion may have been crushed, but the ideals he fought for—the right to live with dignity, the freedom to choose one's path, and the courage to stand against injustice—are victories that cannot be undone. His spirit lives on in those who continue to challenge the forces of oppression, proving that even in the darkest of times, hope can be a powerful weapon.

The Flame That Cannot Be Extinguished

In the end, Spartacus achieved a form of immortality not through conquest or wealth but through his unwavering commitment to freedom. His story lives on because he showed us that the strength to resist lies within each of us, that no one is truly powerless, and that even a single act of courage can echo through history. Spartacus's life is a testament to the idea that freedom is a flame that cannot be extinguished, no matter how fiercely it is opposed.

The legacy of Spartacus is a reminder that the fight for justice and dignity is eternal, that the human spirit is capable of rising above even the most dire circumstances. Though Rome defeated his rebellion, they could never extinguish the ideals that Spartacus embodied. His memory lives on as long as there are those who believe in the power of freedom, who dream of a life beyond oppression, and who are willing to stand together in defiance of injustice.

Spartacus's story has been told and retold across the centuries, evolving with each generation but retaining the same essential message: that the pursuit of freedom is an inherent part of the human condition, a cause worth fighting for, and a light that will never fade. The flame of Spartacus burns still, inspiring all who seek a world where every individual is free to live with dignity and purpose.

Final Words: The Immortal Legacy of Spartacus

Spartacus's life and legacy are a testament to the power of one individual to inspire change, to transform lives, and to ignite movements. His name has become synonymous with courage, his actions a symbol of the fight against oppression, and his memory an eternal reminder that the desire for freedom is a flame that can never be extinguished. As long as there are those willing to resist, to hope, and to believe in a future free from tyranny, Spartacus's legacy will endure.

In every generation, there will be those who look to Spartacus as a source of strength, as a reminder that even the mightiest powers can be challenged, and that every act of courage has the potential to change the world. Spartacus's rebellion may have ended on the battlefield, but his ideals live on, a beacon of hope for all who continue the fight for freedom.

As we remember Spartacus, we honor not only his struggle but the struggles of all those who have followed in his footsteps. His legacy is ours to carry forward, to keep alive, and to pass on to future generations. For as long as there are those who seek justice, who stand up for the oppressed, and who believe in the power of unity, Spartacus's spirit will remain an indomitable force in the story of humanity.

In the end, Spartacus's true victory was not in battle, but in the legacy of freedom and defiance he left behind—a legacy that reminds us, in every age, that the desire for freedom is a flame that can never be extinguished.

ABOUT THE AUTHOR

This book was created with the assistance of artificial intelligence (AI).

The content within has been generated and refined through the use of advanced AI tools and technologies to ensure accuracy, comprehensiveness, and clarity.

While every effort has been made to provide valuable and reliable information, the use of AI means that this book should not be considered a substitute for professional advice.

Readers are encouraged to consult with healthcare professionals, therapists, or other qualified experts for specific guidance related to their personal circumstances.

Thank you for understanding and for choosing this book.

Ciro Irmici (Spartaco_94_)

Made in the USA
Coppell, TX
24 February 2025